D1571584

Published in Western Australia
by Sandpiper Press
2 Prowse Street, West Perth, W.A. 6005

First published 1992

Copyright © R.L. Woldendorp

This book is copyright.
Apart from any fair dealing for the purposes
of private study, research, criticism or review,
as permitted under the Copyright Act,
no part may be reproduced by any process
without written permission.
Enquiries should be made to the publisher.

National Library of Australia
Cataloguing-in-publication data
Woldendorp, Richard Leo, 1927
Sandpiper Press
ISBN 0-646-09386-X

Colour separations by The Colour Set.

Printed in Western Australia by Kaleidoscope.

Typeset in Western Australia
by Image Communications, West Perth.

Film processing by Churchill
Colour Laboratories.

3

JOURNEY THROUGH A LANDSCAPE

RICHARD WOLDENDORP'S AUSTRALIA

This book is dedicated to

my wife Lyn and our daughters

Yolanta, Gemma and Eva

FOREWORD.

Australia is a land of patterns but too few of us ever see the shape and symmetry created by nature or carved by man. Aboriginal artists, who now command international recognition for their work, have long studied and recorded the patterns in their lives.

Richard Woldendorp is a rare European-Australian who has created a new art form from the patterns of our country. His creativity with a camera, and his ability to turn what to some observers is a simple landscape into a work of art, places him among the greats of Australian photography.

I have been an admirer of Richard's work for many years. Like him, I have been fascinated by the patterns of the land, patterns I see when visiting outback pastoral properties, but which I have been unable to capture on film.

This book highlights the best of Richard's work. It is a delight to study and marvel at how the eye of the artist can create an object of beauty from something as mundane as plastic pipe on the side of a freeway, an industrial rubbish dump or an aerial view of a salt stockpile.

It is his aerial work which best sets Richard apart from other great Australian photographers such as Max Dupain who used the human form for his raw material.

Seen from the air, through the lens of Richard's camera, Australia takes on a different form. He has created a new way of looking at our country and for that his work will stand the test of time.

Janet Holmes à Court.

Janet Holmes à Court, Perth, Western Australia. 3 April, 1992

RICHARD WOLDENDORP IS SEEING THINGS.

My friend, Richard Woldendorp, is sitting in my kitchen overlooking the garden and I'm wondering what he sees out there that I don't.

I once wrote about him suggesting that this photographer saw things differently from the rest of us. You can use the same camera, with the same film stock and the same lens and shoot the same scene at the same moment – his picture will finish up on a gallery wall; you'll get a snap. I've tried it. I know.

He looks for all the world like a rather friendly middle-weight boxer: short, thick-set, still hard, with the athlete's muscles close to the surface. He boxed a bit in the Dutch Army while doing his national service in Indonesia. It's not hard to imagine looking into his shrewd eyes over the top of a pair of five-ounce gloves.

As a journalist, I have worked with him on many assignments, mostly in the outback of Western Australia. Travelling with Richard, you always have the feeling that you are going to arrive safely, no matter how hazardous the journey might be. He would be a good man in a tight spot.

In fact, he is an ideal travelling companion: tough, thoughtful, resourceful, good-natured, witty and filled with insights he is always willing to share about his angle of vision on the fascinating world around us as you journey. The fact is, this tough-guy has the soul of a poet and the eye of an angel.

Years ago, at the time when Richard had just discovered in himself his passion for photography, my partner and I, who were running a small advertising agency, gave him his first commercial jobs. He was, at the time, earning a living as a house-painter. Those first pictures told us that house-painting was about to lose a practitioner.

So, how do you get to go from house-painting to exhibiting your stuff in international galleries? Here's how Richard tells it:

"My first job in Australia was working for a painting contractor. Studying commercial art in Holland I'd learned a little bit about paint and mixing paint. With my limited English it was probably the only thing I could do at that time."

He worked for someone else at first, then branched out on his own.

"After five years I decided that I needed a holiday and I went back to Holland. In those days you went by ship, and like any good tourist, I took a camera with me and shot photographs along the way. Some six weeks later I arrived in Holland and had the black and white films processed. Looking at the proofs, I was quite impressed with what I had captured and in the way I had interpreted the various scenes I had encountered. After a couple of months taking more photographs in Europe, I decided I wanted to become a photographer. Before then, the idea had never occurred to me."

For several years, as he learned his craft, Richard shot all manner of pictures for our agency until, at last, he was able to make a living doing the kind of work he wanted to specialise in – exploring the unique face of Australia.

He always gave us the impression that he might be good at most things that took his fancy. When, later, he and I worked together on two documentary films, the same level of talent surfaced at once. It was the first time he had ever used a movie camera, an old clockwork Bolex with a three-lens turret we bought secondhand. A few hundred feet of filmstock through the camera and – apart from being constantly and spectacularly seasick (we were shooting a film about the life of a crayfisherman and Richard's talents do not include being a sailor) – he was in his element.

Looking now at the lovely images he captured on those long-forgotten projects, it is clear that, had Richard decided to become a film cameraman, he might readily have succeeded in that field to the same degree he has in still photography. It is typical of his capacity to focus that, even although he was fascinated with the possibilities of the moving image, he made a conscious decision at that time to stay with still photography.

No one arrives at the level of skill Richard has achieved without influences. Ernst Haas was an early one. Richard once had the good fortune to be invited to spend a month in New Zealand in the company of this old master. As Richard recalls: "Being with him was inspiring and rewarding – one of the great highlights of my life. Haas conveys his philosophy very lucidly, both in his work and in his written word. And he was so capable of conveying his love of mankind in his work. It was so obvious in his whole attitude. He gave four, or five different lectures about his approaches to photography – and about his life, people he had met and had been influenced by, places he had been, the various ways you could approach a subject – it was a great experience."

Now other photographers are equally impressed with Woldendorp who has built an international reputation for his work which is displayed in galleries in Europe and the United States as well as in Australia. Elsewhere in this book Richard Woldendorp discusses his philosophies. He talks of "capturing the reality in an abstract form." How well he succeeds!

Max Dupain, Australia's renowned photographer, recognised the unique talent of Woldendorp after seeing it for the first time in a collection of Australian work in the Macquarie Gallery, Sydney. "We don't seek information in the brooding aerial abstractions of Richard Woldendorp; they delight the eye as beautiful symbols of the Australian landscape and indulge our senses in enough mystery to last a lifetime. Yet they are not a denial of actuality.'

The images he captures of Australia – especially those from the air – go beyond the realms of photography. He brings to his work the sensibility of a master landscape painter, and fuses that with a remarkable technical skill that is now as natural to him as breathing.

Observing Richard Woldendorp's images, Professor George Seddon says: "one of the most striking features of them is the clarity: of focus, of light, of composition, but most of all, of perception. There are no hesitancies, nor doubts about these images; they are pared down to the bone – simple, clean and harmonious."

But in which direction does a photographer go to develop his art; especially one whose work is already refined to what seems an ultimate degree? Richard admits to being at a bit of a crossroads in this respect. He wants to maintain his interest in photography while developing his craft to his own liking. He senses a need to further refine his 'seeing,' or to apply some further technical change to assist him in moving in new directions.

He says, "I'd like to extend my work in the direction of fine art. Nowadays, most artists do not see any separation between photography and art. Other photographers are using altered states and manipulated techniques to enhance the creative range of photography:

David Hockney, Lucas Samaras, Jan Saudek and others have all made their personal stamp on modern photography. I also admire Sam Haskins for his subtle variation in double exposure and juxtaposition. So far, I am still a straight shooter, mostly because I lack the technical skill, but I am doing some experimental work in double exposure and movement. The latter produces some fascinating, painterly results with optical reality.'

Not a small ambition: deliberately adding to photography the dimension of captured time. To Richard, the challenge is not unrealistic. He says, "It just takes conviction to stay with the idea long enough to develop a technique you need to bring it off.'

Knowing Richard's attitude – and that's a word he uses again and again – he will bring it off. His work is never an accident. It is the result of immense physical hard work harnessed to a thought process and skill that has been refined by years of single-minded passion for his craft. He brings to his work a clear intellectual rigour. One thing you notice about Richard Woldendorp: when you ask him a question, he thinks before he speaks. You might describe him as the thinking man's photographer.

He says, "Right now nothing is sacred. Everything is possible. Videotape shows that anything that can be imagined can be captured, visually. The willingness of the video imagemakers to go to any lengths to gain their effects comes back on us photographers – challenging us.'

This collection of Richard's photographs, "Journey Through a Landscape", is his most personal to date – there's obvious passion in every image and clear evidence of his almost childish sense of wonderment. Looking at these pictures we have the privilege of sharing the unique point of view of an artist who clearly recognises the incredible variety and beauty of Australia's unique landscape.

As a writer I sometimes doubt the truism that 'one picture is worth a thousand words.' Seeing these pictures, I'm willing to concede.

Bill Warnock, Perth, Western Australia. May 1992

JOURNEY THROUGH A LANDSCAPE.

"The photographs in this book show a personal point of view of the natural and man-made landscapes of Australia. Most of them have been taken from the air; an appropriate viewpoint for such a huge and often inaccessible continent.

"After years of photographing in Australia, it occurred to me that I needed another vantage point to make sense of the scale of the Australian landscape. The immensity of it becomes apparent from above. The moment you get up in the air, your horizon extends much further and you can clearly see the natural and the man-made happenings in that landscape. The freedom of shooting from the air gave me another point of view. By taking out the horizon one is left with nothing but the structure of the landscape. My choice was opened up dramatically. I suddenly realised I could choose an abstract design, but still leave the strength of the reality – be it a coastline, sheep tracks, plough patterns or salt flats.

"The modern generations of Australians have grown up with the camera and the plane – two tools that come together harmoniously. Now we can all see our country from the air. Air travel, plus the clarity of the skies gives us a shared vision of our landscape. Australia is the most worn down continent. The flatness of the terrain from the ground view rarely shows us the vastness of the continent and the way it has evolved. In other countries, high mountains give you a feeling of perspective and distance and your point of view changes continually as you travel up and down the landscape, more so than when you travel along a flat plain. I feel the aerial perspective compensates for the lack of mountains.

"The Australian landscape is varied; however, great distances have to be travelled before a change is noticeable. The Northern Kimberley landscape is very different from the areas around Esperance, or the forests of the South-West, or the interior of the Great Sandy Desert, but the changes are spaced over enormous distances. Driving through it, the variations are not obvious immediately, but flying over it you can clearly observe the changes from one area to the next."

1. Lake Argyle.

2/3. Tidal flats, Kimberley coast.

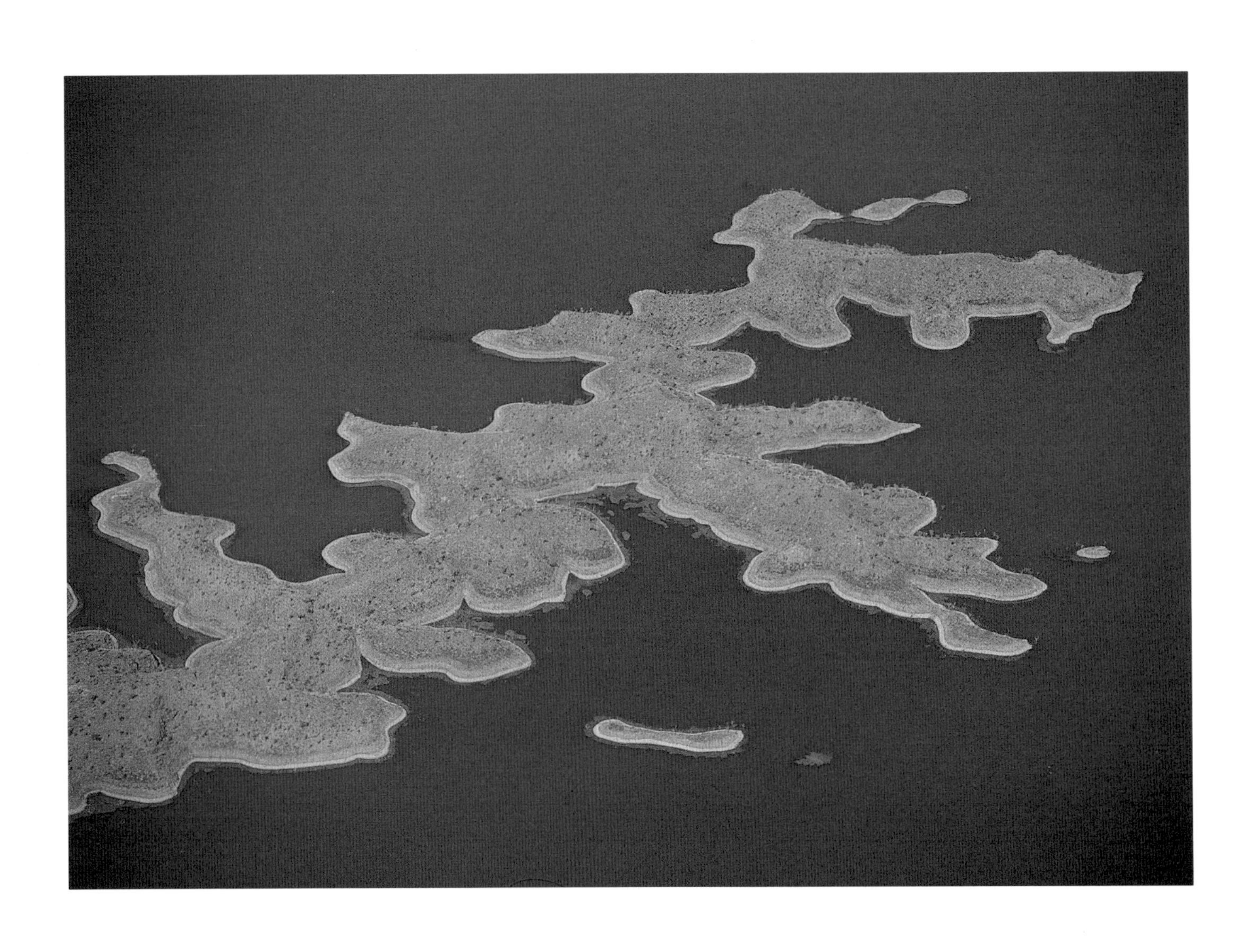

4/5. Two images of Lake Argyle.
Pristine islands and drowned trees.

6. Corellas over a backdrop of pandanus.

7. Magpie geese, Ord River.

8. Boab trees, Carlton Station.
9. White gum in a sea of cane grass.

10/11. Two faces of folded landscape, Carr Boyd Range and Ragged Range.

12. The domes of the Bungle Bungle.

13. Erosion pattern near the Northern Territory border.

14. Overleaf: Craggy Kimberley landscape.

15. Ragged Range.
16. Carr Boyd Range.

17. Southern slopes Ragged Range.

18. Pitt Range.

19/20. Mangrove coast, Kimberley.

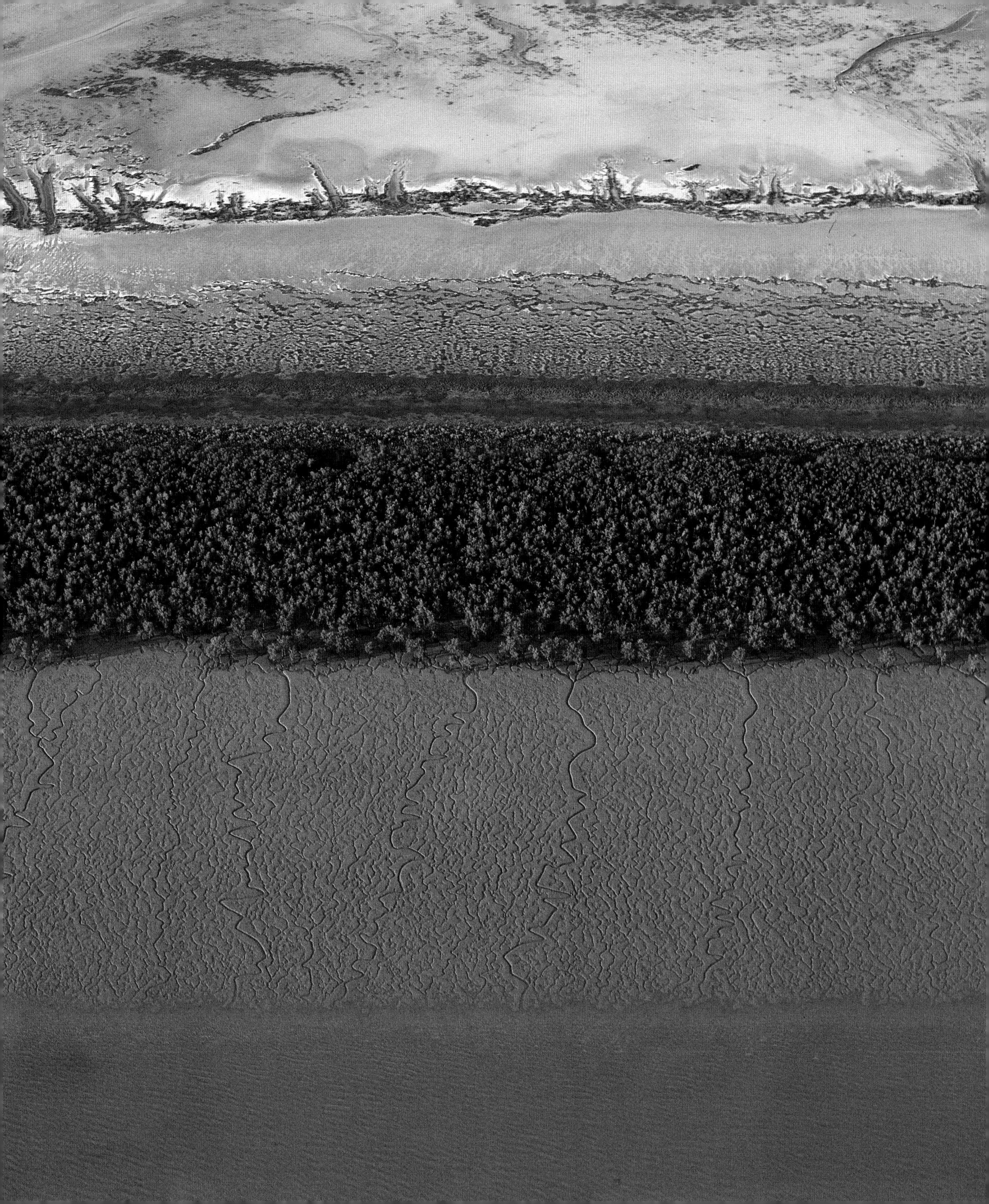

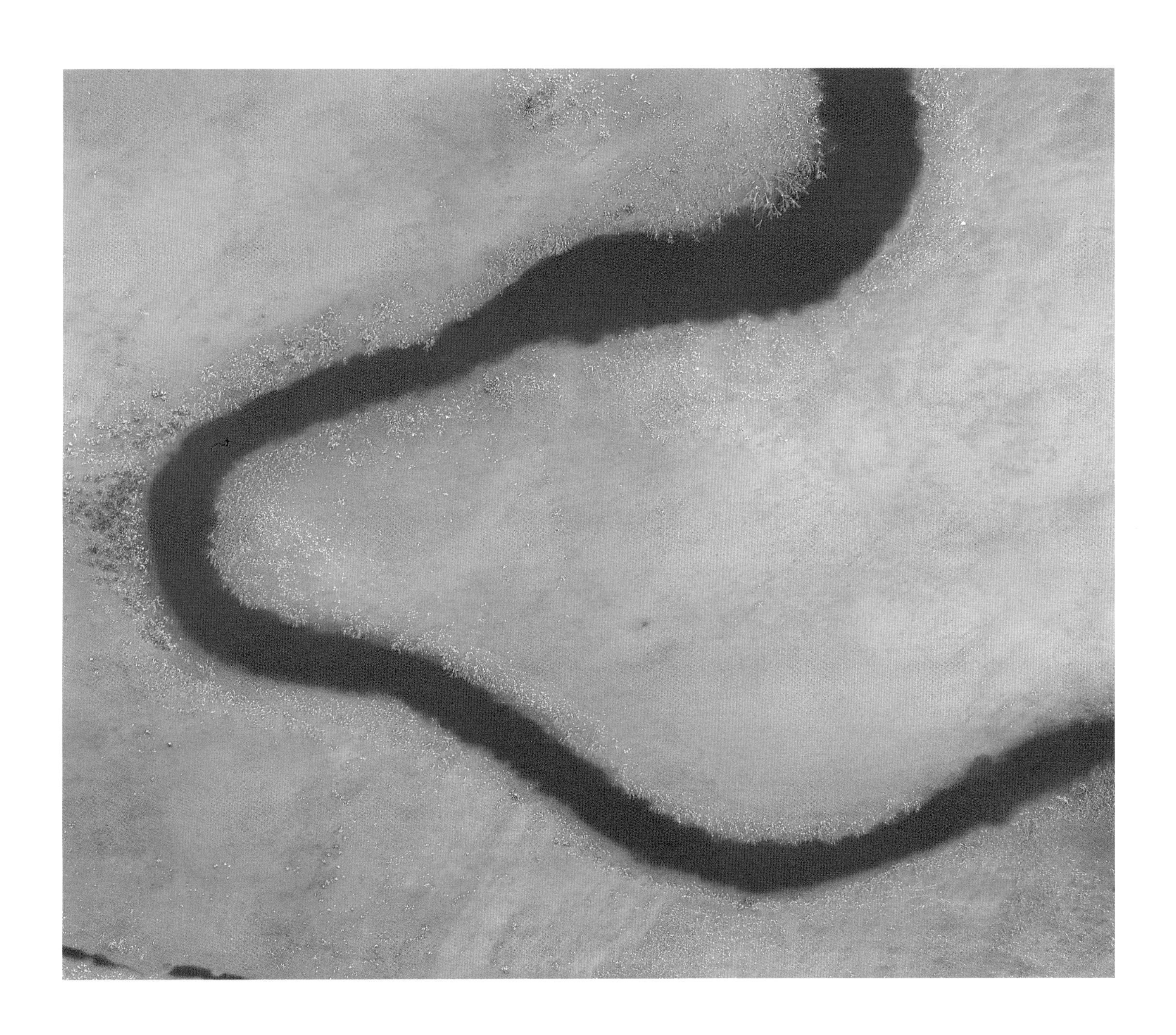

21/22. North coast waterways.

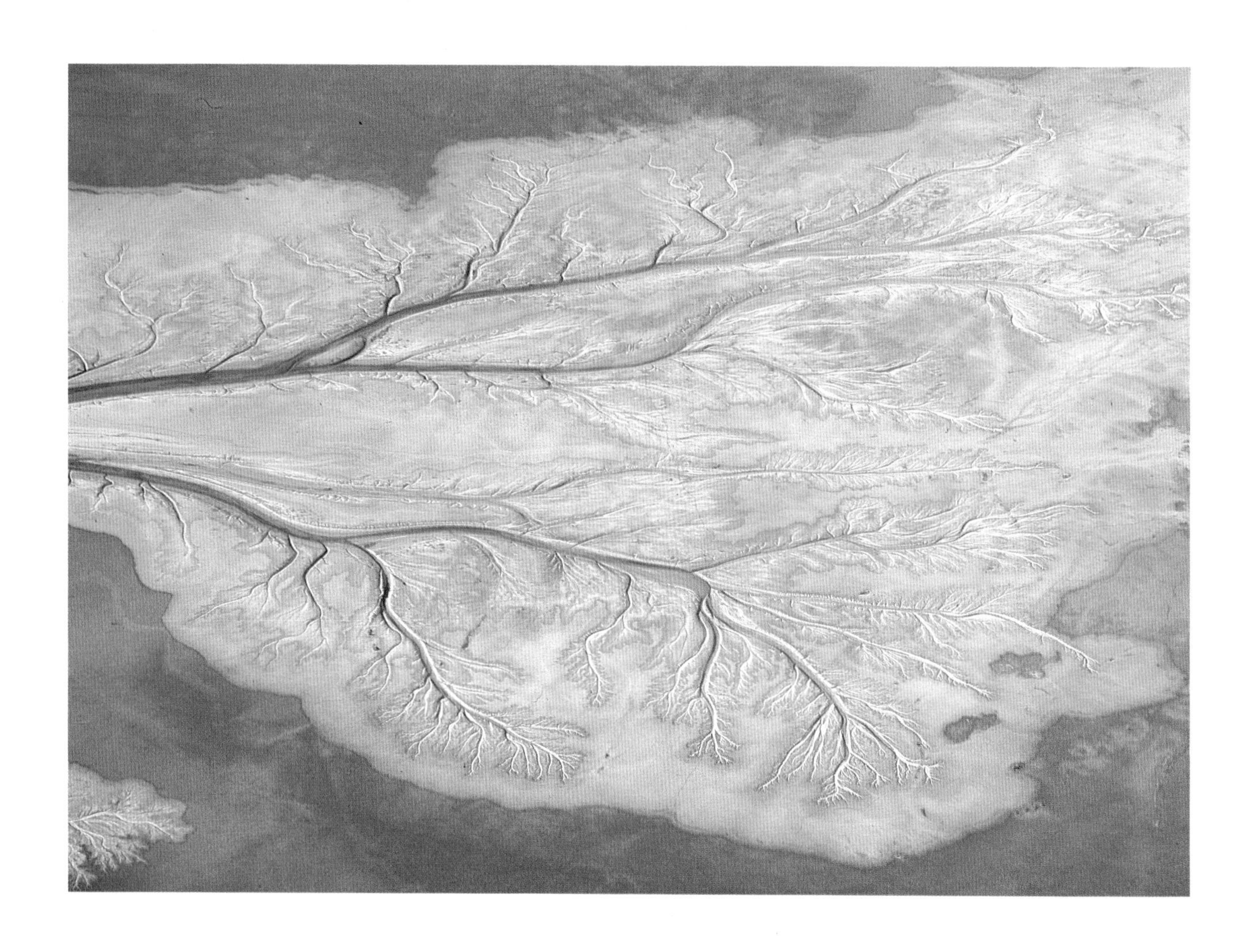

23/24. Tidal flood plains, Derby.

"It requires a lot of hard work to develop one's own style in order to make a statement that is different from others who may see the same things and use the same equipment. The art of photography is to learn to 'see' and understand the techniques involved in order to transfer a three-dimensional reality to a two-dimensional picture. It is not easy to make a picture worth looking at. Most people are only interested in recording a certain event, or in keeping a record of a particular happening. A photographer must use his, or her talent to make something outstanding. The most rewarding aspect of photography is in recognising one's own individuality and expressing it artistically.

"It usually takes me a couple of hours to tune into a specific landscape, to lose my inhibitions and start to see the pictures around me. It's the physical being of the landscape I'm aware of when I travel through it, or over it. It's a combination of looking and seeing – two different things – particularly in a natural landscape. Landscapes surprise you. Things can happen. The unexpected happens. Going through a landscape is always an adventure. I feel walking is about the right pace to develop an intimate association with a landscape.

"The way each individual interprets a scene is unique, but if you turn a corner and there is an obvious photograph – a waterfall, a mountain, or a stream – chances are that everyone is going to photograph it. And the majority of people will take virtually the same picture. What can you see that is different? It is a matter of developing your own unique point of view. It gets back to having the right attitude. This is one thing you can change and is part of one's own creative make-up. There is an enormous amount of good pictures out there, whether you see them or not – you are the only limitation.

"You can go through the same landscape twice and get different results if you are willing to change your point of view. If you don't see the pictures, you don't get them. Changing your attitude gives a totally different result. For instance, you can approach a subject at ground level, from the air, at various times of the day, or even with a particular technique in mind. All these approaches give different results."

26/27. Claypans in the Ashburton River area.

25. Previous page: Dappled rock near Paynes Find.

28/29. Spinifex landscapes, Pilbara.

30/31. The great variety of Hamersley Gorge.

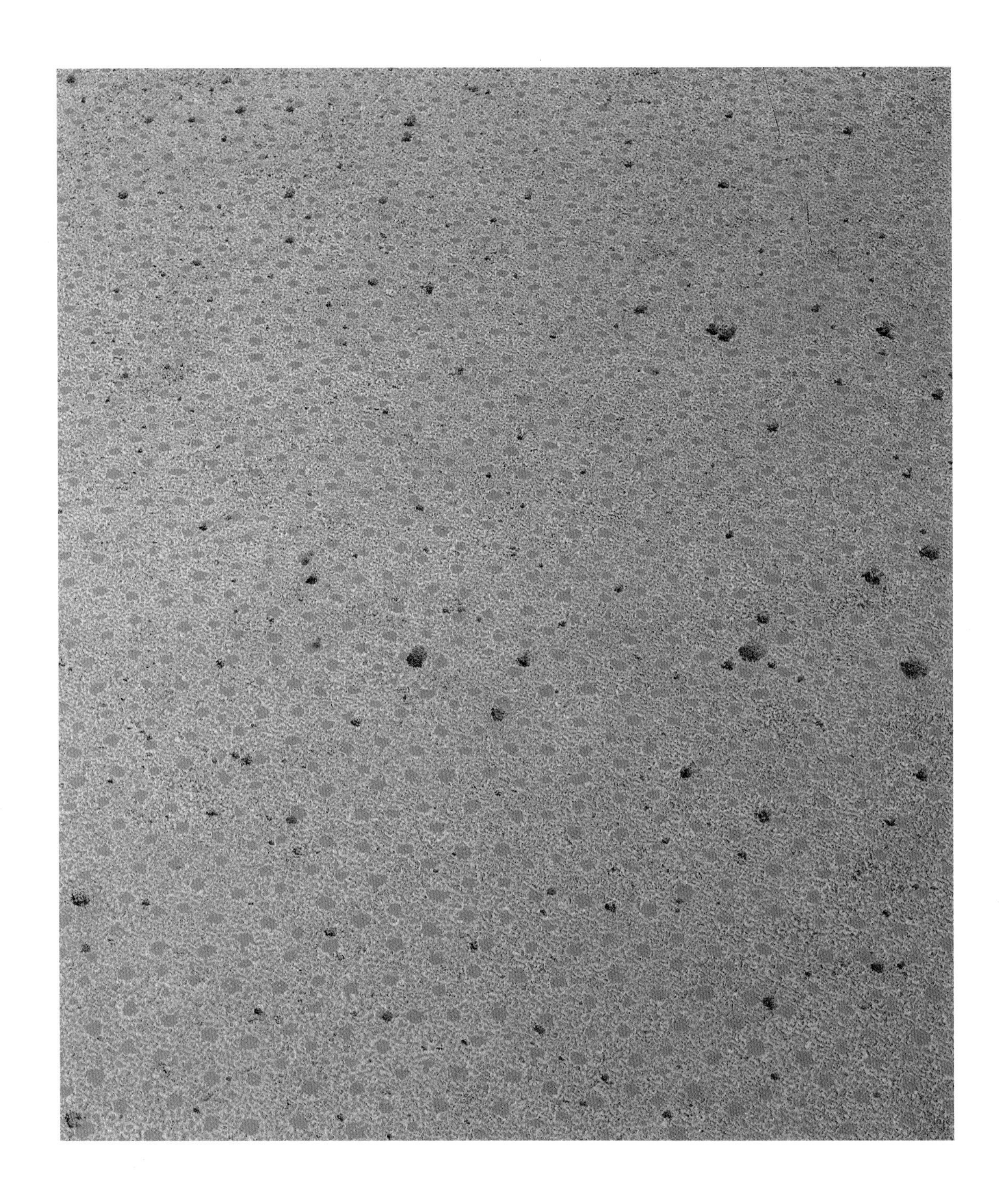

32. Ant clearings.

33. Dunes, Great Sandy Desert.

34. Rocks and grass texture.

35. Spinifex at twilight.

36. Pelicans, Lake McLeod.

37. Egret in a tidal swamp.

38. Overleaf: Corellas, Fortescue River.

39/40. Water over rock surfaces.

41/42. Dry inland rivers, Ashburton and Rough Range.

43. Flood plain near Mt Newman.

44. Stony gibber plain near Paraburdoo.

45. Trees in the Kimberley.

46. Scrub country, Murchison.

47. Monger's Lake.

48. Everlasting wildflowers near Mundiwindi.

49/50. Triangular pools in the Pilbara and Darling Range.

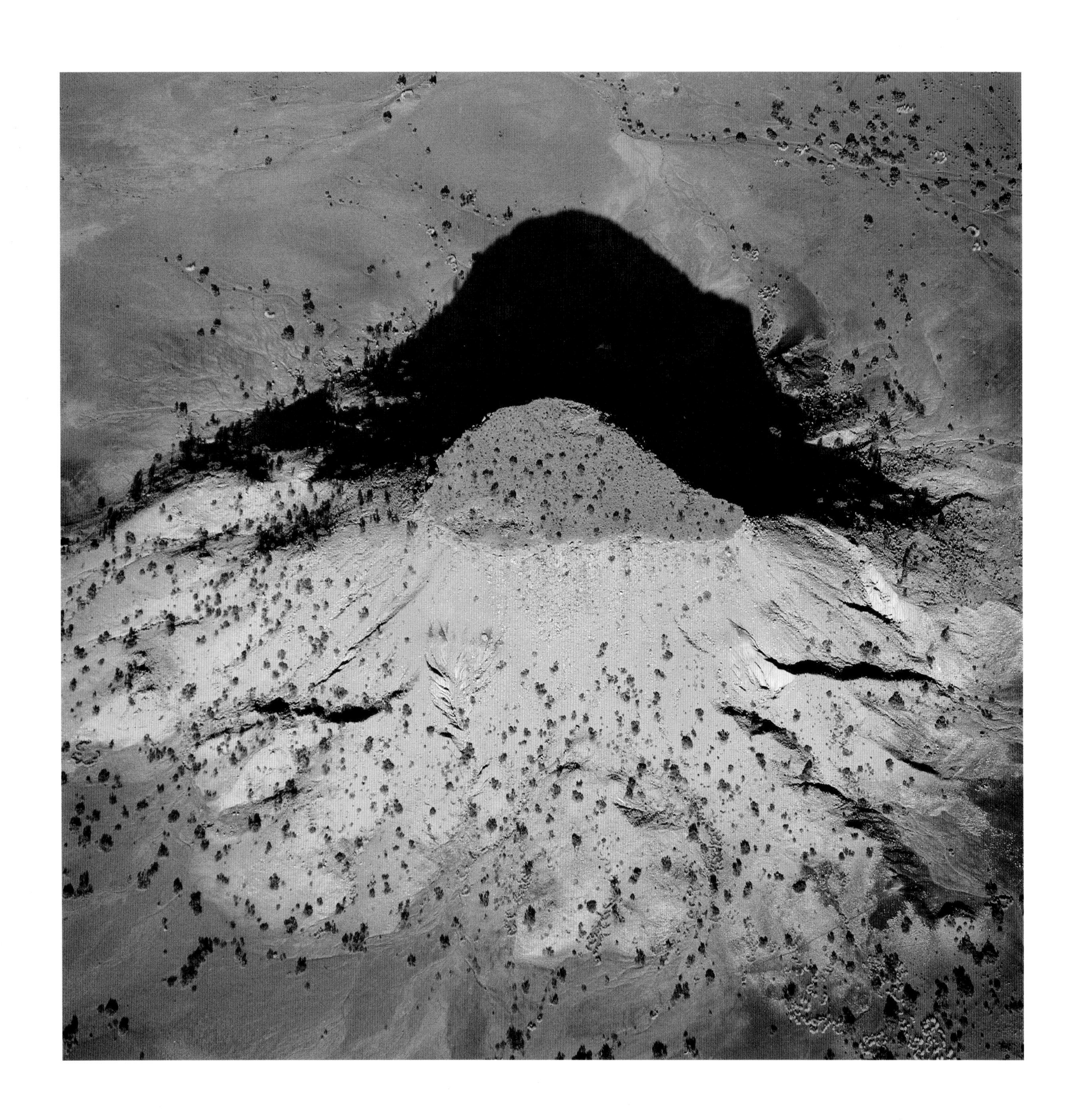

51/52. Two aspects of worn down tablelands in the Pilbara.

"When the first Europeans came to Australia, their artistic interpretation of the landscape was through European eyes. They did not always portray the flora and fauna as it was, but rather as how it ought to be, according to their training and previous experience.

"Aerial photography has assisted painters such as Fred Williams, John Olsen and Robert Juniper to understand the complexities of the land viewed from above. Their portrayal of the stick-like flora and the bones and sinews of the landscape is well known.

"Unlike the painter, the photographer, by pressing the button on the camera, will get all the elements of a scene within the frame: all of it sharp; all of it visible. In a complex scene, the photographer gets too much information.

"The painter, on the other hand, starts with a blank canvas and paints, draws the lines, and adds on until he is satisfied. He can alter or control the amount of information he gives. The photographer starts with a complete optical reality within the frame. With the right approach and selection, he can maximise the impact of that landscape by eliminating detail and, at the same time, strengthening the elements he wishes to portray. There are a few shots in this book which illustrate the simplicity that can be achieved by photography and make a very pronounced statement about that particular landscape. I try to intrigue and entice the viewer.

"A landscape can be photographed many different ways, from many different angles, but Cartier Bresson's 'decisive moment' also applies to aerial and landscape photography whereby the angle of the approach and the quality of the light combine to give us the strongest image. It is the recognition of that decisive moment that provides the picture.

"The aspect of aerial photography that I particularly like is that the view from the air is so unpredicatable. I don't always know what I'm going to see. And then there's the watching for that one moment when the landscape and I come together and I see something – some scene I want to say something about, that is specifically my own, and unique; something that captures the essence of the situation."

53. Kangaroo, Burrup Peninsula.

54/55. Dunes near Eucla and Lancelin.

56. Coastal scene near Dongara.
57. Dune, water and sky.

58. Play of sun on dune near Eucla.

59. The Pinnacles, near Jurien Bay.

60. South West beach.

61. Hamelin Pool, Shark Bay.

62. Hamelin Pool.

63. Collier Bay, Kimberley.

64. Broome beach.

65. Ord River.

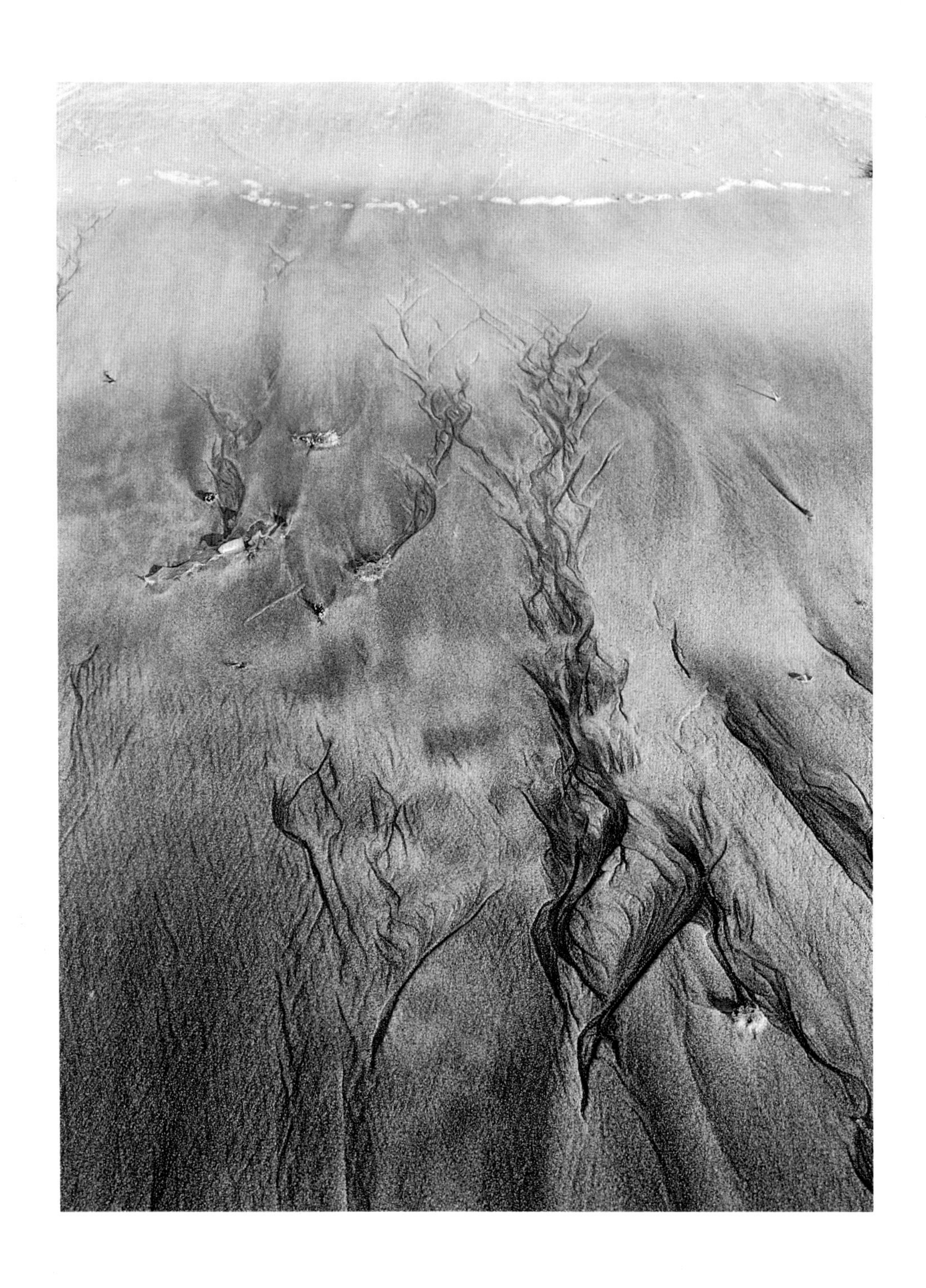

66. Shoreline detail.

67. Geraldton coastline.

68. Overleaf: Boat harbour, South West.

69. Pindan beach, north of Broome.

70. Lancelin coast.

71/72. Coral Bay.

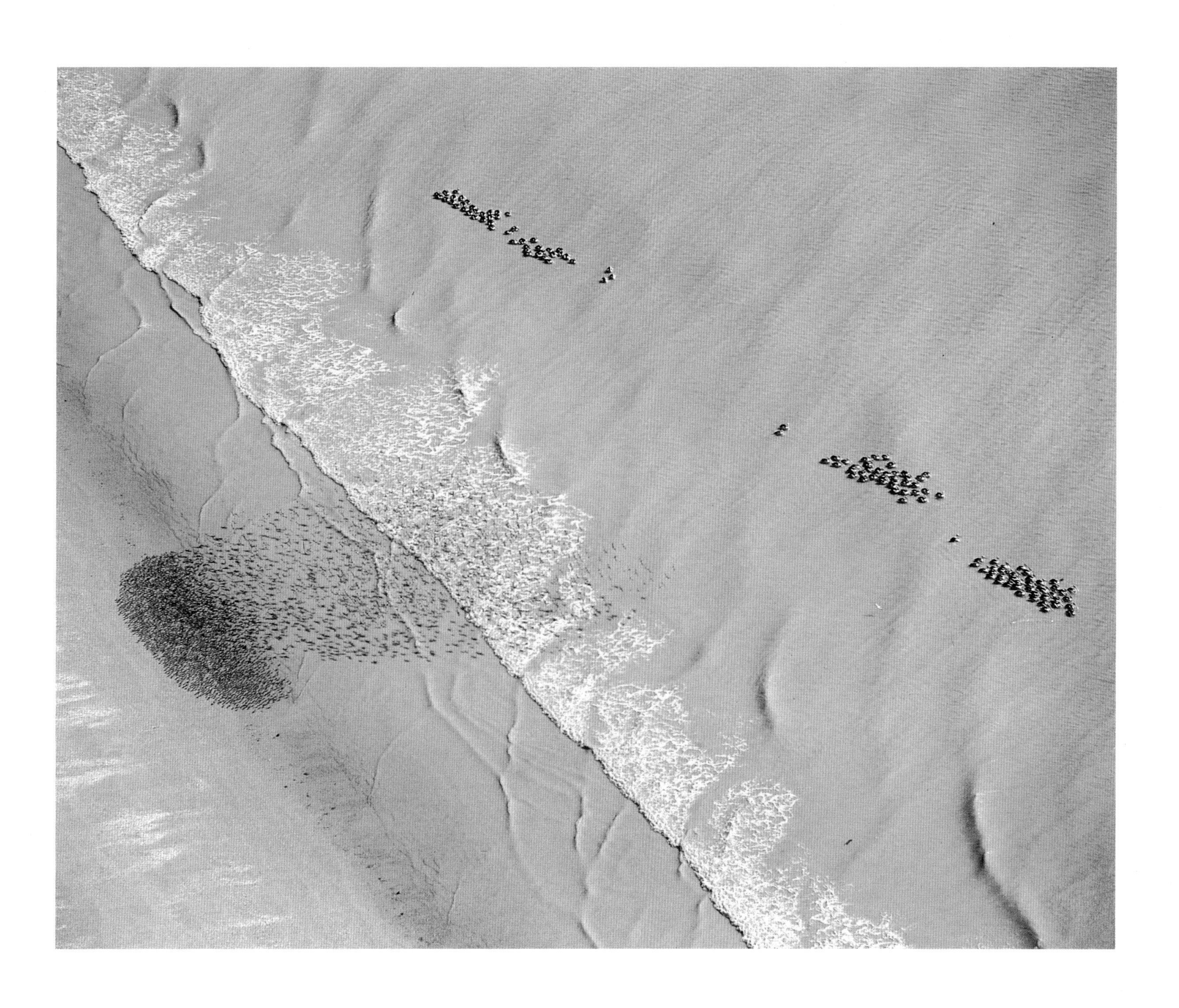

73. Shark Bay.
74. 80 Mile Beach, north of Port Hedland.

75. Seagrass, Shark Bay.
76. Lake McLeod, north of Carnarvon.

77/78. Sand-bars, Fortescue River & Greenough River.

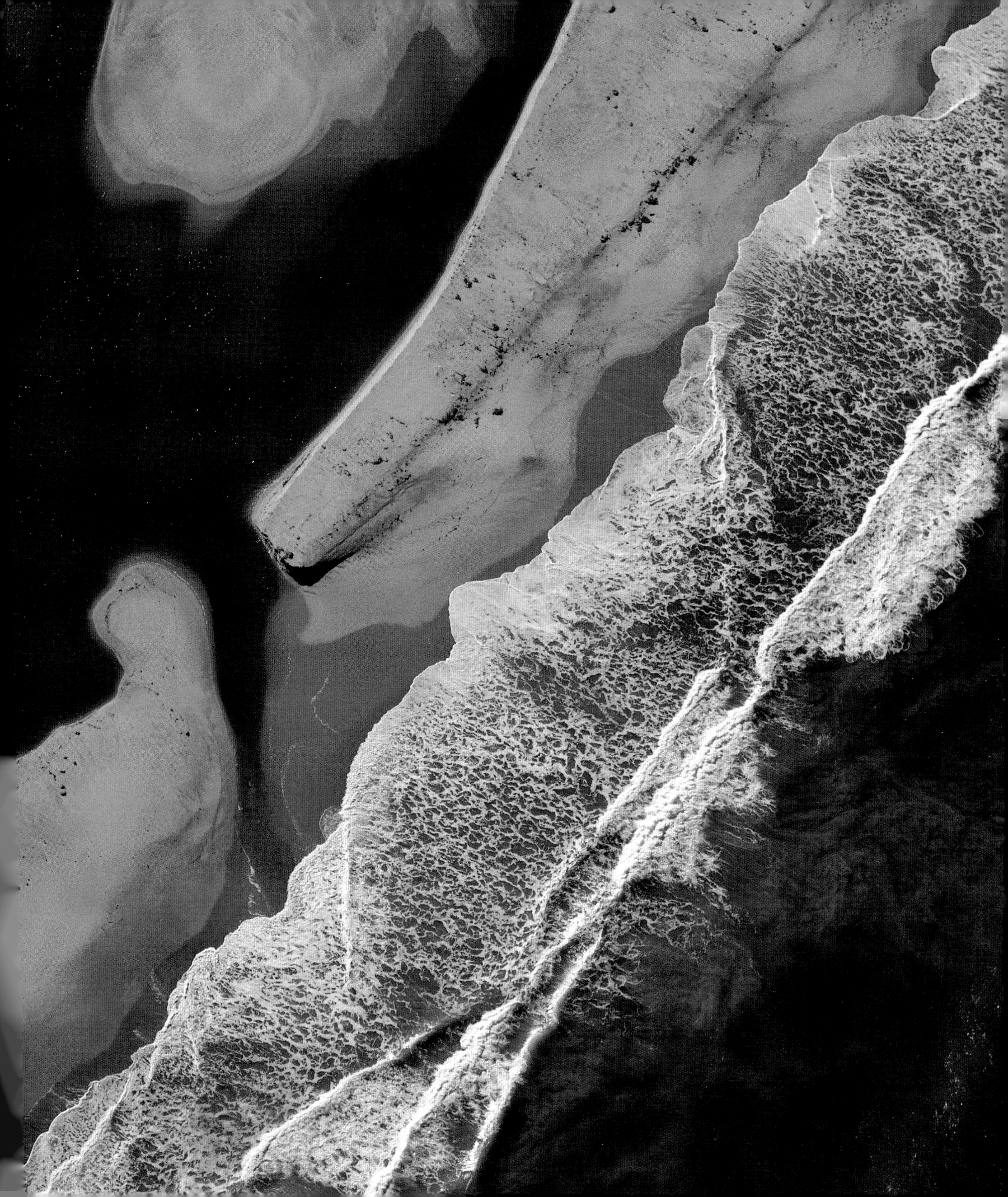

79. Wilsons Inlet.

80. South West coast.

81/82. Salt lakes east of Esperance and Peron Peninsula.

83. Island, Mongers Lake.

84. Lake Lefroy.

85/86. Salt lake, Hyden and Kambalda.

"The Aboriginal people roamed Australia's broad spaces for more than 40,000 years, respecting its systems. Signs of nature guided them in seeking their own survival.

"This was not so with the first Europeans who came to these shores. They gazed aghast at a landscape that, in many ways, seemed to threaten their survival. They tried to deal with it as best they knew how, but their imported techniques, ideas and attitudes were not always in sympathy with the unfamiliar environment, nor with its inhabitants.

"This was the beginning of an uneasy relationship with the land. Two centuries, after all, has not been a great deal of time to mould a relationship between Western man and this 'new' continent. That development has been far more leisurely in other continents. It gets back to something David Suzuki wrote in his foreword to William Line's book, 'Taming the Great Southland.' 'Nowhere on earth has such a large portion of the world been occupied in such a brief period of time.' The speed of impact of Western civilisation on Australia has been extraordinary.

"On a flight from Perth to Sydney one can see, except for the Nullarbor Plains, the endless degeneration of the original landscape for the purposes of farming. Below you lies a never-ending patchwork of farmland. Very little natural bush has been allowed to survive the onslaught. A landscape that took millions of years to shape and establish has been profoundly re-shaped by economic and political expediency. We have, without malice, insulted all that the land is. Through interaction and evolution, nature created a spacious matrix in which life could diversify. If we force it to provide only for us, we must expect to pay the price.

"Travelling through farmland by car one has the illusion of space and freedom but in effect you drive most of the way between two rows of barbed wire. I would have liked to have seen a percentage preserved for flora and fauna to remind us of what was once there."

87. Blackboy forest.

88. Bushfire, Pilbara.

89. Burnt gully near Roebourne.

90/91. Bushfire patterns, central Western Australia.

92. Helena Valley.

93. Fitzgerald National Park.

94. Overleaf: Tracks through burnt landscape, King's Park.

“In this collection of aerial photographs I try to emphasise the beauty of the man-made landscape. Being aware that the landscape is so extraordinary, I want to convey something of this to others. My personal satisfaction comes from recognising the beauty that is there. The results may, at times, border on the abstract, but that is the way I like it. It emphasises some of the characteristics of the land.

“The man-made landscape can also be beautiful – the cities, the roads, the farming patterns, particularly at certain times of the year such as harvesting, ploughing, reaping and sowing. This book contains many such images which remind me of the abstract and cubist painters. If only farmers could see the marvellous images they create as they work their land!

“I have always been fascinated by these images as seen from the air. I'm primarily interested in the visual quality that these man-made landscapes can provide. Industries and cities provide very graphic images. Good examples are the strong geometrical designs of the solar salt and mining industries. The designs of squares, parks and streets are more obvious from the air, giving a good indication of their role in the environment.”

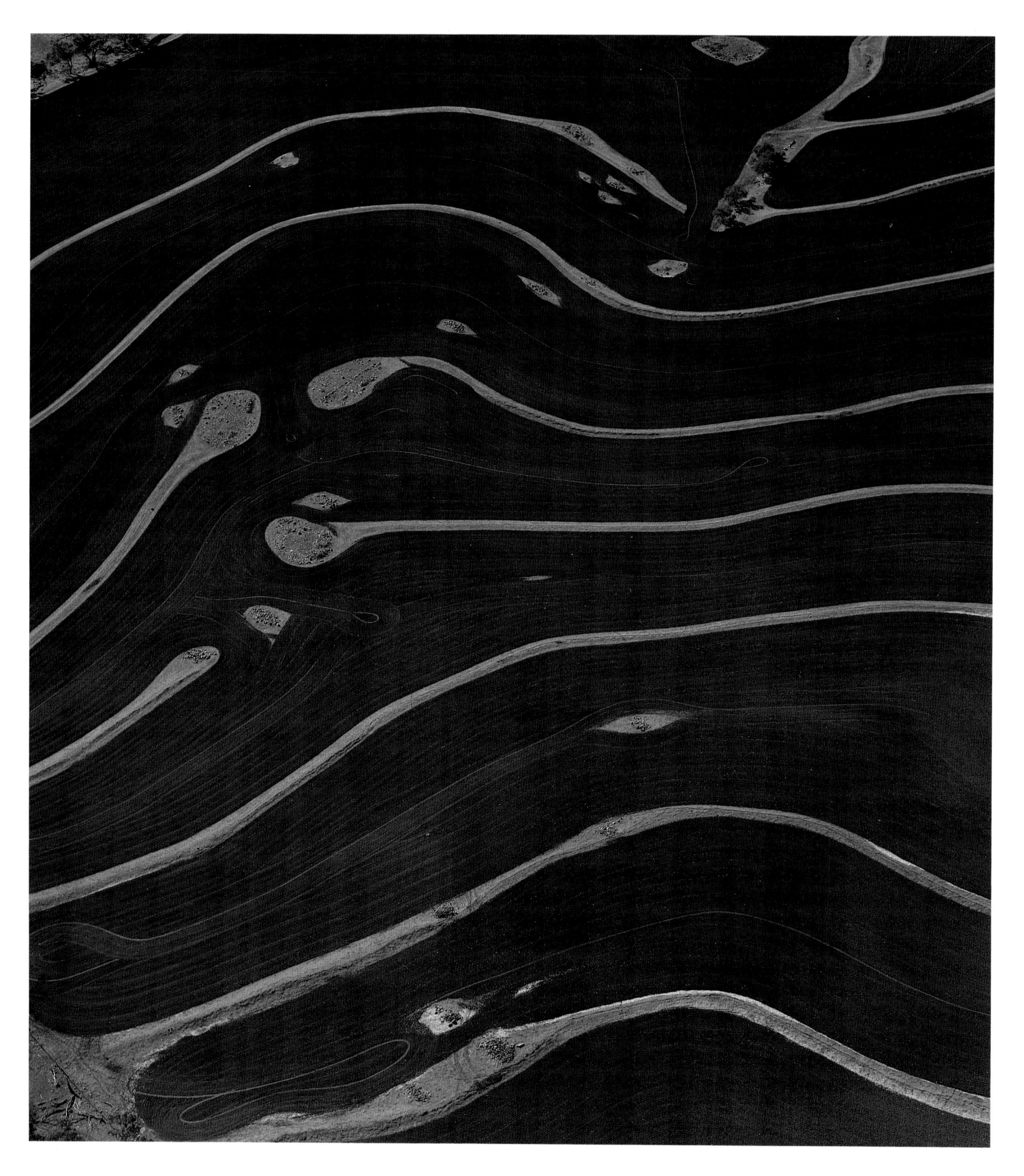

96. Contour ploughing, wheatbelt.

95. Previous page: Plough patterns.

97. Channels leading to dam.

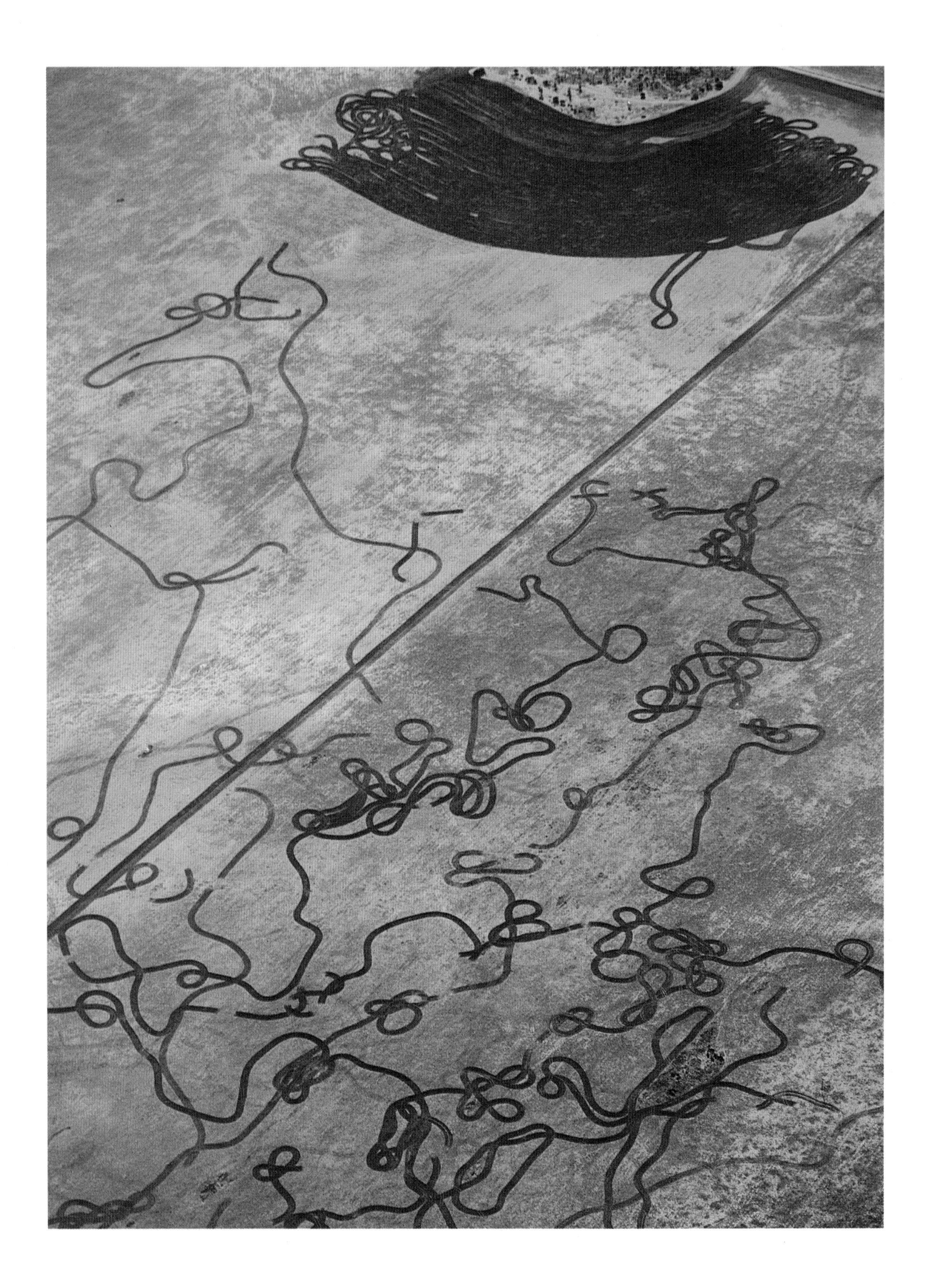

98/99. Ploughing, Mullewa and near Northam.

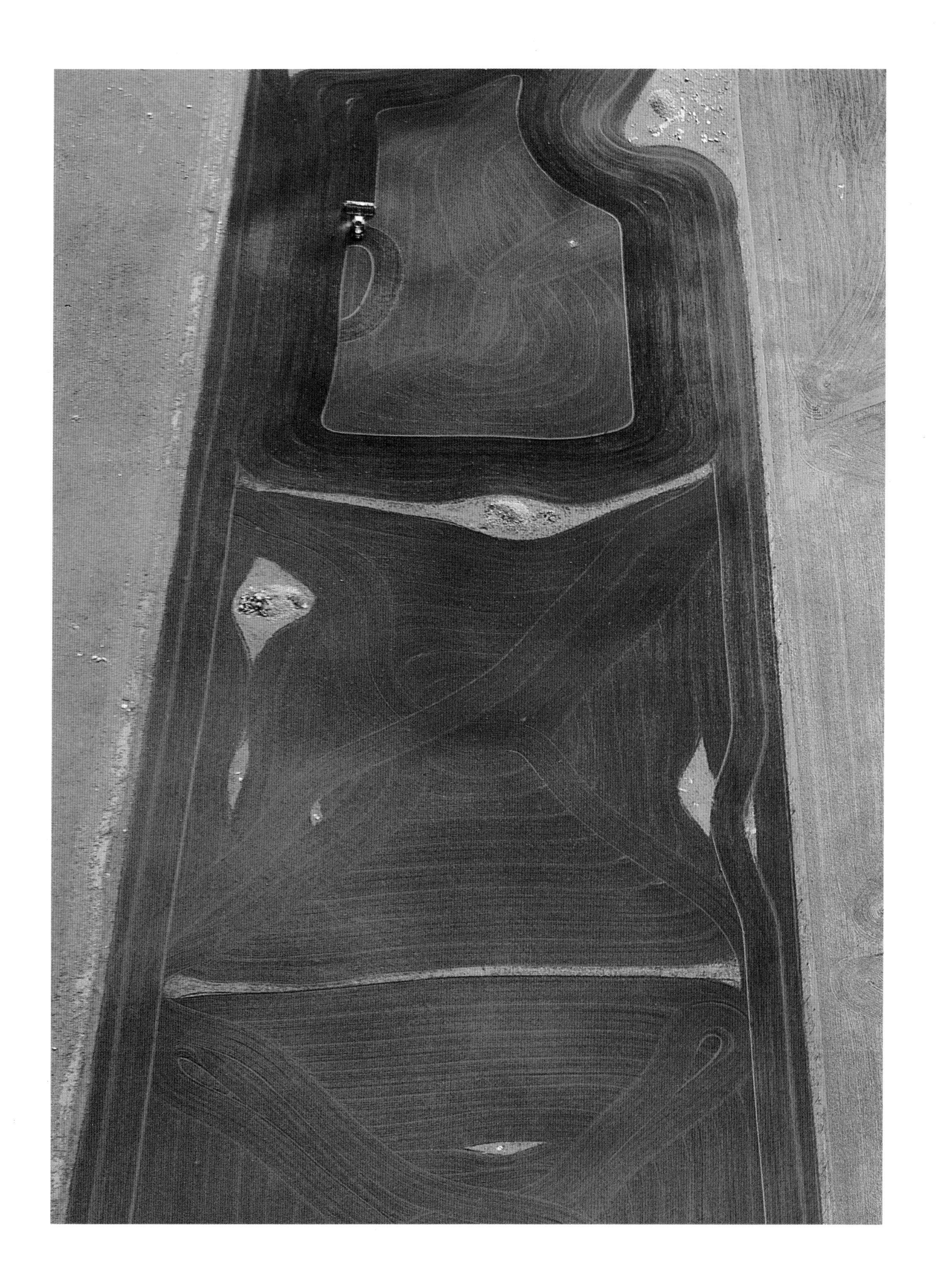

100/101. Ploughing, Northam.

102/103. Plough patterns near Grass Valley.

104/105. Harvested wheatfields.

106. Dam in wheatfield.
107. Cutting hay near Geraldton.

108/109. Wheatfield near Cunderdin.

110. Stock-yard, Kimberley.

111. Fields near Dongara.

112. Overleaf: Contour ploughing.

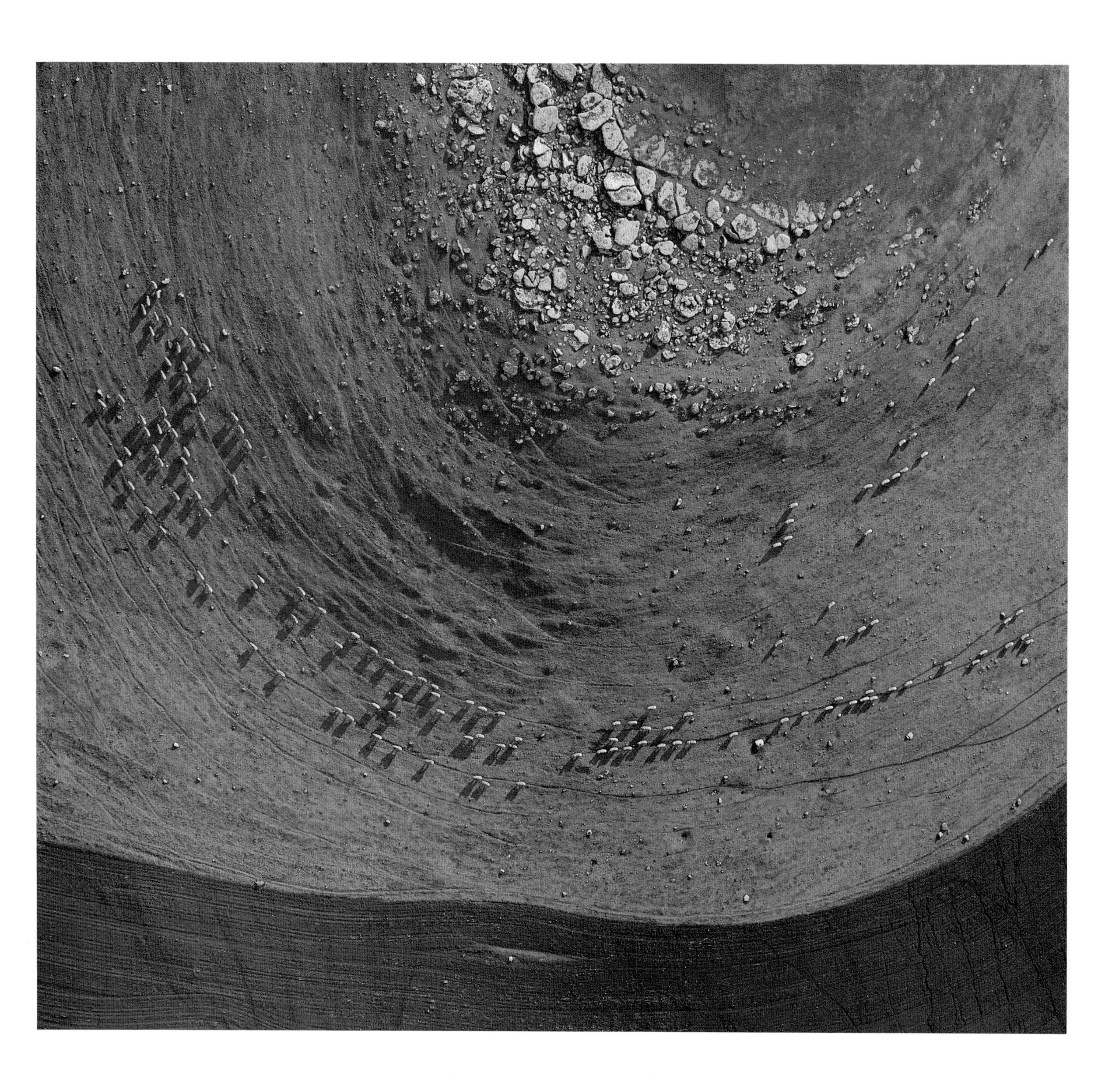

113/114. Sheep tracks near Greenough and Beverley.

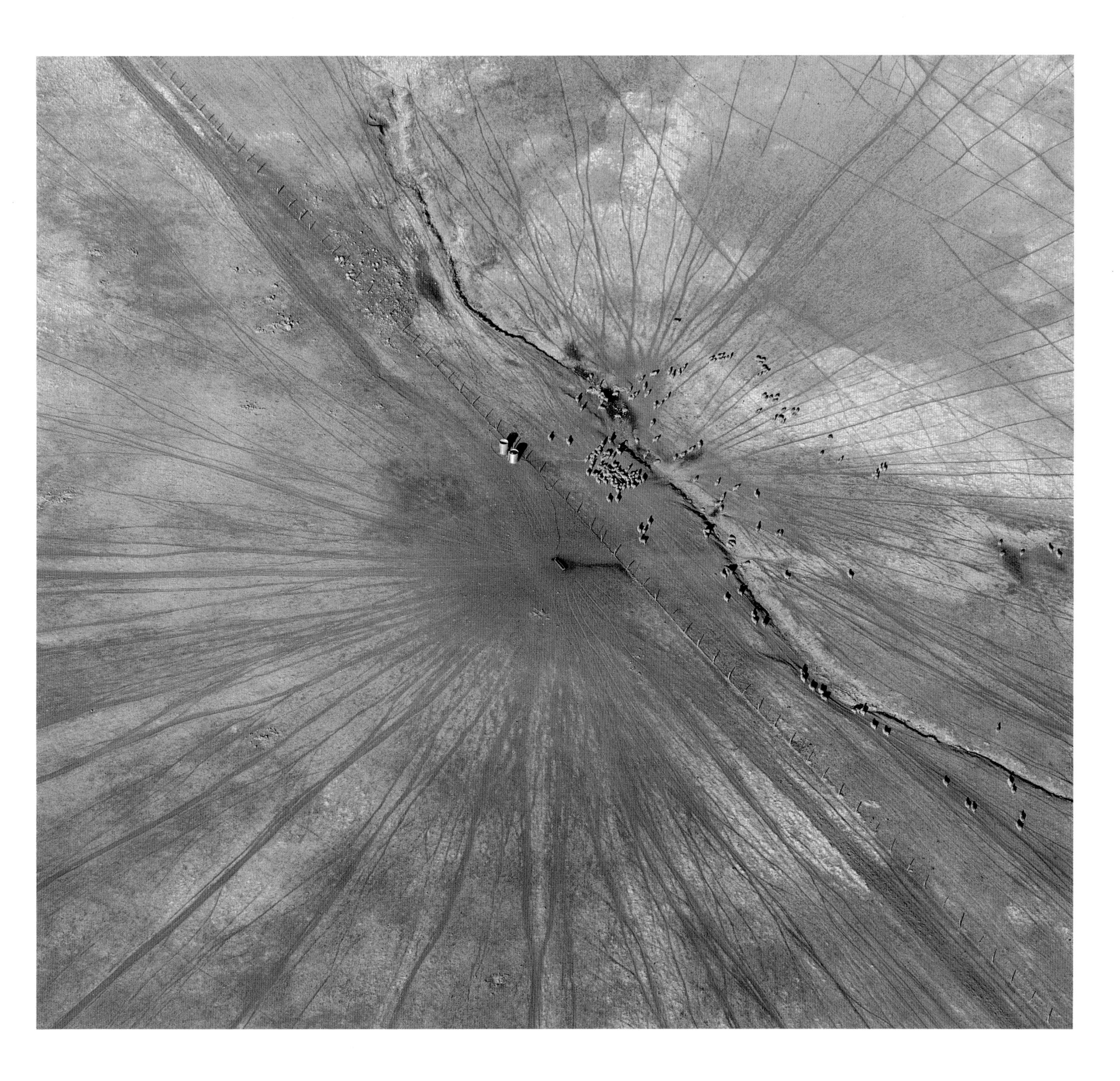

115/116. Dams in wheatbelt.

117/118. Circular irrigation, Kimberley and South West.

119/120. Ord River landscapes.

121/122. Vegetable growing near Perth.

123. Paddocks accentuated by trees.

124. Bottom of an oil tank.

"Colour, in nature, is never a disturbance, nor a distraction. When I walk in a natural landscape, I am looking for details that make an interesting statement about that particular landscape. Colour is the key. There is a constancy in its occurrence. Green of trees and growing things; blue of sky; red, brown, or yellow of earth, or rock – these are the primary hues by which surfaces in nature can be read. Thus, colour becomes a way of orienting ourselves in the natural world. There is something soothing in this.

"Because of this background constancy, any variation becomes significant. Colour differences separate and indicate subject matter in a scene (as in the photograph of Greenough rivermouth where layerings of colour denote the different territories of river, dune, beach and sea). But it does much more than this. Colour variations can make us aware of seasonal differences, time of day, space and distance. It can also signal a departure from the usual, as when a bushfire reverses the palette from green to black, or grey.

"Colour changes in nature is the way I become alerted to whatever features are in that landscape. Against the background of what is known, expected, or predictable, new elements stand out. It might be a parrot, a flower, a sunset, an animal; it might be a flight of corellas over a pandanus plain, or an egret on a tidal swamp. Colour signs are the way in which I see what is there, select and balance my images.

"In the man-made world, colour is often used quite indiscriminately. It may be used to emphasise the unremarkable. Frequently it is overstated, thus confusing the viewer. It is an unreliable guide to the relative importance of things. It bombards the retina with messages that are often frivolous and irrelevant.

"In situations where colour becomes confusing I prefer the use of black and white photography to retain a graphic and less confusing image. However, when I photograph nature, I work in colour since it is an intrinsic element of whatever I perceive. Not only does it direct my seeing with its samenesses, shifts and differences, but it is the essence of the photographic rendering of my vision."

Richard Woldendorp, Perth, Western Australia. 1 May, 1992.

126/127. Solar saltworks with truck, Dampier and Lake McLeod.

125. Previous page: Balloon shadow on morning mist.

128. Farm fence on a salt lake.

129. Watering system, Freeway.

130. Tyre tracks on a salt lake.

131. Goldmine, Coolgardie.

132. Iron ore waste dump.

133. Equipment yard, Burrup Peninsula.

134. Bauxite residue ponds.

135. Iron ore quarry, Cockatoo Island.

136. Yachts, Swan River.

137. Yacht Club, Fremantle.

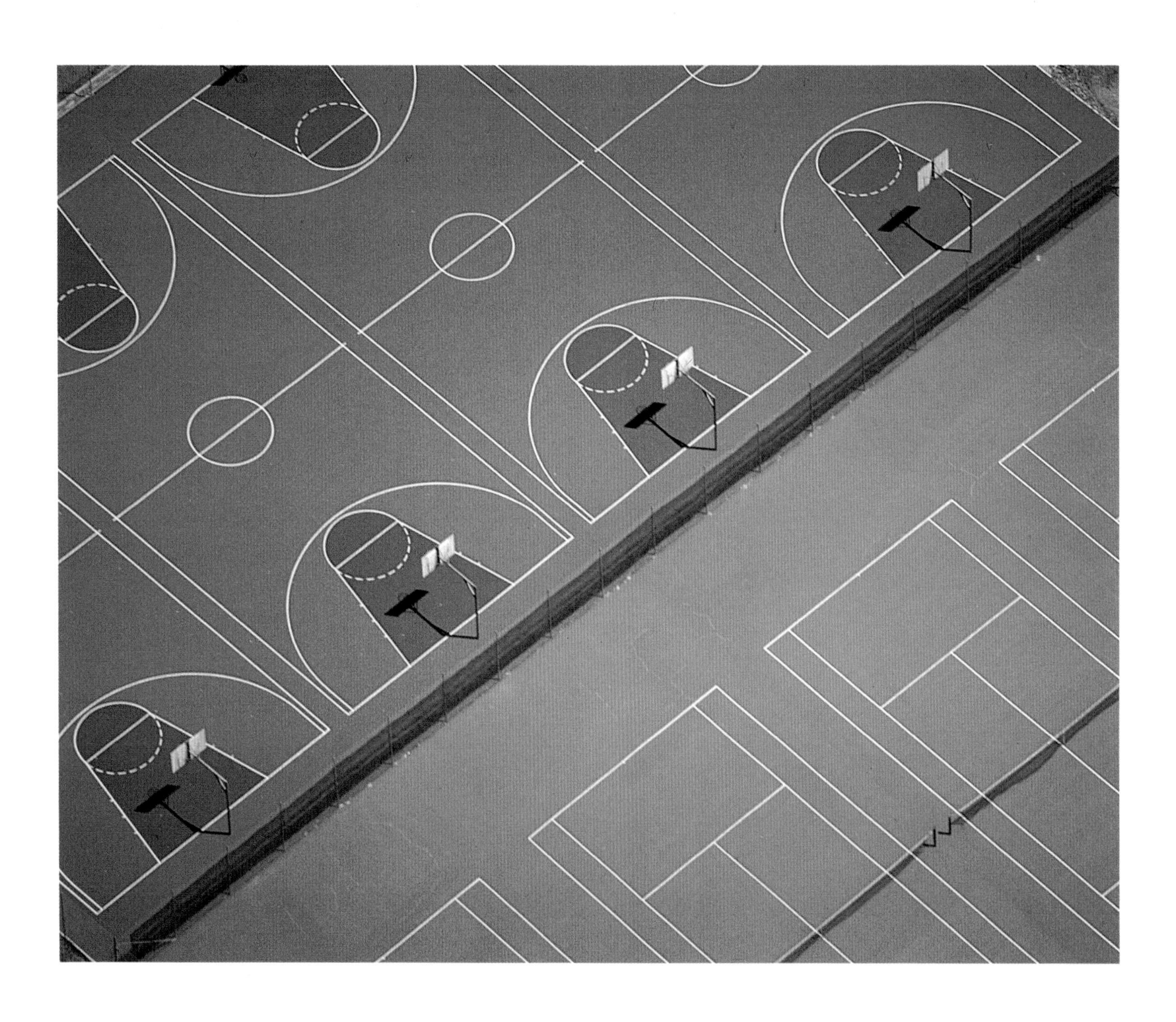

138. Tennis court off-sets netball court.

139. Suburban development.

140/141. Two resting places.

142. Overleaf: A festive pattern of people.

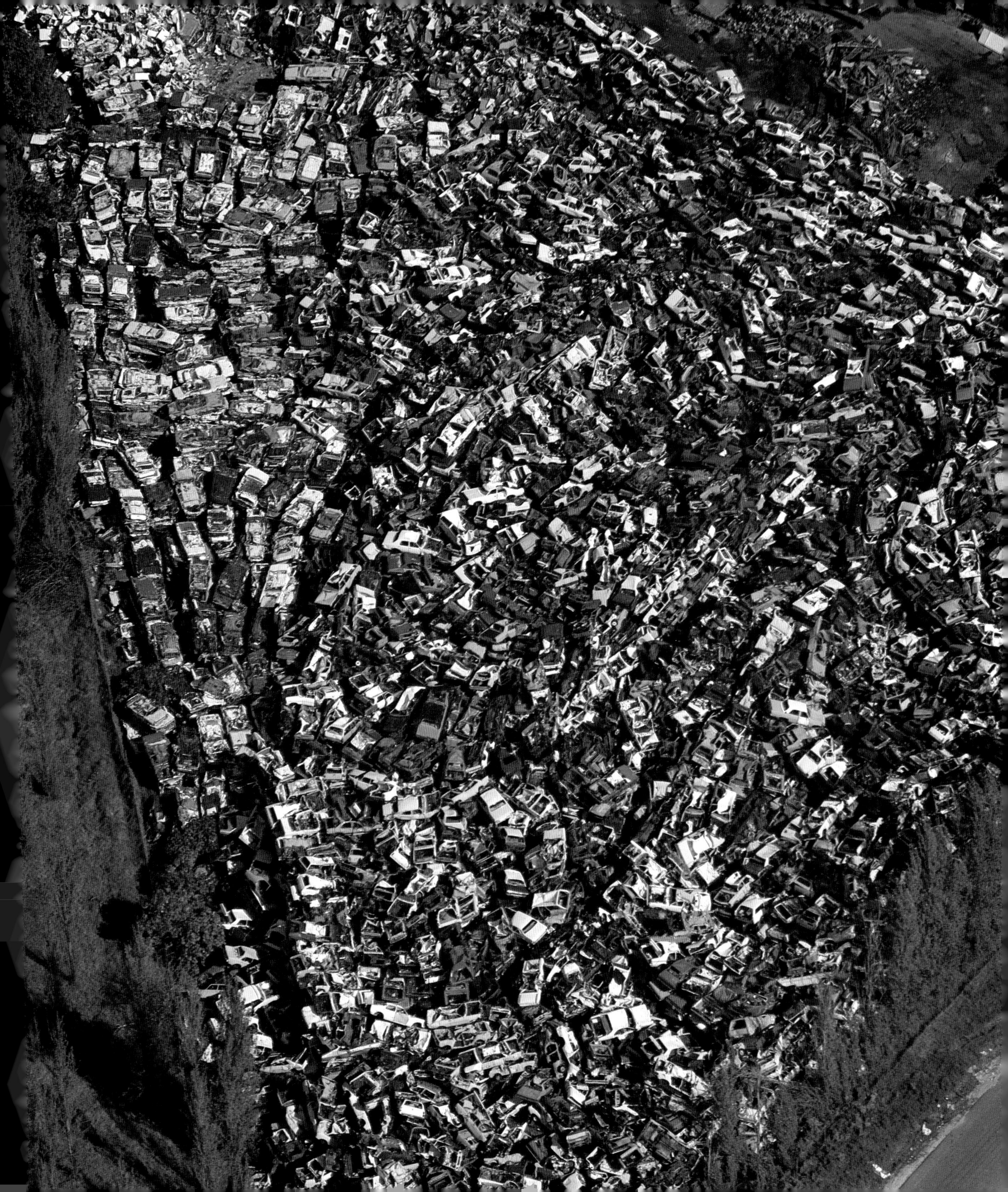

NOTES ON THE PHOTOGRAPHS.

1. I liked the soft shady textures of Mt. Brooking with Lake Argyle in the background.

2/3. These pictures of tidal flats were taken near the Northern Territory border, where the tidal variation can be as great as nine metres. This huge fluctuation in water levels creates ever changing patterns which can be best appreciated from the air.

4/5. Lake Argyle is a vast, inland, man-made body of water, resulting from the damming of the Ord River. The islands in these pictures have a pristine aspect still, as they have not yet adapted to the new abundance of water.

6. Flocks of corellas are a constant presence in the north and their sighting, although common, never fails to impress.

7. Magpie geese, here shown against the light as they take off from the Ord River, are seasonal visitors, mainly seen during the "wet".

8. The boabab or "bottle tree" is peculiar to the north and may be seen across the continent as far as the Queensland border.

9. During the "wet" cane grass explodes in a growth spurt that can take it as high as two metres. The slender tree trunk in its midst is that of a "snappy" white gum.

10/11. Early morning light falls on the Carr Boyd Range. On the right the southern slopes of Ragged Range are caressed by a late afternoon sun.

12/13. The spectacular region of the Bungle Bungle has not long been open to tourists. Its sandstone domes are the result of weathering processes over long periods of time. This particular form of eroded landscape occurs elsewhere in the north, however, as shown by the picture on the right, taken near the Northern Territory border.

14. I am fascinated by the endless variety of the Kimberley landscape. Since much of the terrain is now readily accessible by air, this variation of rock, structure and vegetation can be seen and appreciated in a relatively short space of time. As seen from above, it is a continual source of inspiration to me.

15/16. The shadows cast by early morning light accentuate the folds of Ragged Range, while on the right, late light strikingly illuminates the Carr Boyd Range.

17. The gentle slopes of the southern part of the Ragged Range are accentuated by the tree line on top of the ridges which in the bright sunlight reminds me of the pastel quality of a watercolour.

18. Soft patterns of growth follow the lines of an ancient eroded landscape. This was taken from an oblique angle at about 2,000 metres.

19/20. Mangroves form the bastion of the Kimberley coastline, protecting the land from encroachment by the sea. Receding waters leave their marks upon the shore.

21/22. Waterways wander through flat landscapes. The aerial perspective reveals the complexities of tidal variation and its effects. The greater the rise and fall, the more varied the landscape becomes. I am always intrigued by these fluid changes.

23. A leaf-like patterning formed by a network of water channels.

24. Silken designs emerge from the waterwave workings of the tide where the Fitzroy River enters King Sound.

25. The pattern of this rock near Paynes Find in the Murchison seems to echo the dappled effect of the clouds.

26/27. "Claypans" is the term often used to denote a variety of residual salt lakes and flood plains in the outback. These two views are of such formations in the Ashburton region and near Shark Bay.

28/29. Spinifex is a supreme plant adaptation to a harsh environment. The highest concentration of this semi-desert plant occurs in the Pilbara region of Western Australia where, in certain areas, it is the only thing that survives in the rocky and dry landscape.

30/31. I find Hamersley Gorge one of the most interesting in the Pilbara. There is always variety to be seen in the layered rock strata as it catches the light. And water is always a welcome sight after the dryness of the surrounding area.

32. This aerial photograph was taken east of Newman, where the Great Sandy Desert begins. The circular patches are actually ant clearings. Later when I drove through this region I examined them at close range and found that the ants clear the spinifex in approximately five metre circles taking the grass underground. The patches appear to be territorial and are evenly spaced over a wide area.

33. The parallel ridges of the Great Sandy Desert run due east-west. I was impressed by the vast extent of this area which changed little during my four hour flight in a Cessna 172, between Newman and Halls Creek.

34. Rocks and grass blend in a uniform conglomerate paving, typical of the North.

35. This photograph was taken after sunset, hence the beautiful soft light and subtle detail of this spinifex and rock landscape in the Chichester Range.

36. I took several photographs of this group of pelicans but I chose the one against the light because of the unusual pattern created by light and shade.

37. To me the egret is one of the most beautiful of birds – elegant, aloof and very much an individual. Here it provides a striking contrast, seen against the reddish swampland of the Pilbara coast.

38. This flight of corellas over a dry creek bed along the Fortescue was taken from approximately 300 metres, looking straight down. In the picture it looks as if the bank of the river is the horizon, with the flock of birds flying through a brown sky.

39/40. Water in a dry landscape makes a particularly strong statement.

41/42. Thin outlines of vegetation indicate the occasional watershed in the Gascoyne River basin (41) and Rough Range near Exmouth (42).

43. The pattern is created by the pressure of water on the vegetation during the annual flooding near Mt Newman.

44. Another variation on the theme of the relationship between plant growth and the availability of water. Thin lines of vegetation stand out against the stony gibber plain south of Paraburdoo.

45. In the Kimberley with its higher rainfall, one can often observe a very even distribution of growth, as indicated in this photograph taken near the Oscar Range in late afternoon light.

46. Growth pattern north of Meekatharra. It is low scrub with occasional grass and is sparsely distributed over the whole area.

47/48. Once a year when the rains have been plentiful the landscape explodes into an abundance of flowers. Everlastings in the

Murchison region in particular are a fascinating spectacle occurring late August-September. 47. One of the bare hills on Mongers Lake contrasts with the carpet-like wealth of everlastings.

49/50. Two triangular bodies of water. The blue one in the Pilbara is created by a particular point of view, and the other in the Darling Range is natural.

51/52. Two indications of a very worn-down tableland. 51 shows the smooth, even rounding of a hill with its spinifex cover. 52 is an aerial of a tableland hill top accentuated by shadow. Both are typical of the Pilbara.

53. The kangaroo appears miniaturised amongst the gigantic boulders so typical of the Burrup Peninsula, near Dampier. This is one of those lucky shots one always hopes to get.

54. I always find dunes a rewarding subject. The play of sunlight over the sands, determined by the time of day and the amount of cloud cover, accentuates the features in a way that never fails to interest me.

55. Early morning light lines the ridges of dunes north of Lancelin. Using an aerial perspective, as I have here, has enabled me to take full advantage of the effect of the low-level lighting.

56. Two strong colours – the blue of the ocean and the green of paddocks isolate the white of a dune near Dongara.

57. Simplicity is achieved by eliminating all unnecessary detail in this photograph but the essence is there. I like saying as much as possible, and strengthening the impact, by providing the least amount of information.

58. The play of light caused by clouds throwing ever changing shadows across the dunes at Eucla.

59. Seen from the air, this landscape of the Pinnacles, Nambung National Park, is reduced to a subtle variation in colour and form.

60. The simplicity of the beach quietly reflecting the blue sky in the receding water, with one of the ever present seagulls.

61/62. One of the most extraordinary areas of Western Australia is Shark Bay – the largest body of sheltered water north of Perth. It has great variety, as is indicated by the following series of photographs. The westerlies which assault the coastline have, in the past, caused many a shipwreck but inland, away from the winds, at Hamelin Pool and the Freycinet Estuary, the shallow, undisturbed waters can be mirror-like. I like to photograph it from the air, as well as from the ground.

63. Looking at the coast. Another quiet area at Collier in the Kimberley.

64. Broome beach with textures created in sand by the retreating tide.

65. I am intrigued by reflections of clouds or trees (or anything else for that matter) in water which is disturbed. Ripples re-arrange the forms and images, and the slight bulging of the water surface acts as a lens that intensifies or decreases colour. This photograph was taken at Lake Kununurra.

66. Seaweed washed up on the shore of a south-west beach.

67. A set of waves approaching the shore. Their lace-like fragmentation on the beach is best seen from the air.

68. This ground level view of water surging towards the shore complements picture 67. The protected nature of the harbour in the south-west where I took this photograph has allowed this beautiful gentle wave.

69. Continuous wave action produces a scalloped effect on a beach near Broome. The red Pindan rock of the coastline forms a stark contrast with the white foam.

70. Here seen in late evening light, this dune stabilised by plant growth is typical of scrub country edging the south-west coastline.

71/72. Ningaloo is a fine coral reef, easily accessible from the coast. These two aerial views of Coral Bay show the variation of colour and form to be seen in its sheltered waters, which are ideal for the observation of live coral and its inhabitants.

73. An aerial photograph showing the edge of Faure Island and the sandbar dividing the ocean to form this layered composition.

74. 80 Mile Beach situated between the Pilbara and Kimberley is a haven for a great variety of bird life. Pelicans in the water and a flock of small birds taking off from the beach.

75. The shallowness and the clarity of the water lets us view the happenings below the surface. The seagrass and the channels are clearly visible from the air with just a touch of white waves on the surface.

76. Lake McLeod, north of Carnarvon, is the result of sea water leaching in to form a permanent pool. Further down the lake the water is used for the extraction of salt.

77/78. Sandbars are ever changing forms due to tidal and seasonal flooding. These two were taken from the air at the Fortescue and Greenough river mouths.

79. Water fanning out through the sandbar at Wilsons Inlet, south coast.

80. Seen from the air the domains of dune, river, beach and ocean stand out in bands of colour on the south coast. The tannin of the forest stains the river brown.

81. Sometimes it is possible to get photographs from a high altitude. I took these many salt lakes north-east of Esperance while on an interstate flight (at about 10,000 metres). Generally conditions are too hazy to ensure this kind of success.

82. Salt pans at Peron Peninsula. The aboriginals call them "birreda" meaning "footsteps of the giants." From the air it is easy to see why.

83/84. Two perspectives of islands in salt lakes. One, at ground level shows a hazy, mirage-like effect produced by hot air and distance. The other is an image of clarity as seen from above.

85. Salt lake showing a limited growth texture on its surface.

86. The swirling effect of water and wind movement creates these patterns on the lake's surface.

87. Regimental lines of a blackboy forest north of Lancelin are highlighted by the late afternoon light.

88-91. Bushfires are a common occurrence throughout Australia. The vegetation in general has adapted to this, and some plants even require burning to regenerate and to reproduce. The patterns portrayed in the aerial photographs 90 and 91 are the result of fires crisscrossing the same area over a number of years. Some of these scars may last up to 100 years before they completely disappear.

92/93. These photographs show the extent of the fire's devastation. Little has been left. The stick-like remnants of vegetation will have to regenerate from the ground up.

94. The skeletal remains of bushland after a man-made fire through King's Park.

95-103. In his seasonal work of cultivating the land, the farmer creates, unconsciously, very strong images. In this section I have endeavoured to give, through a range of aerial views, an idea of the contrasting effects of various farming activities at different times of the year. Because of its geological nature, Australia has its own unique images. George Gerstner in his books "The Farmer, the Artist" and "Flight of Discovery" has used a similar approach in photographing farmlands of Europe and America, yet the pictures he has made differ markedly from these.

104/105. The harvesting of wheat leaves behind impressions very different from the patterns left by the plough. In the wheatbelt of central Western Australia, the vast tracts of open, undulating land allow the clear recording of these variations.

106. Dams, built by man to collect run-off rainfall, are the most common means of providing water for livestock throughout Australia. From the air they can be seen as forming a kind of dotted lifeline over the rural landscape. The various ways the water channels into the dams gives each its own character.

107. This curious pattern is formed by the baling of hay.

108. Sheep create a counter-pattern of tracks when they are set to graze on the stubble after harvesting.

109. The wide range of uses to which the land is put becomes evident from the air. These drying stacks of wheat are to feed livestock. This picture reminds me of an Aboriginal papunya or "dot" painting.

110/111. The juxtaposition of images can highlight similarities of design, as well as differences. What this stockyard in the Kimberley and the plough pattern near Geraldton have in common is obvious.

112. This plough pattern near Toodyay was photographed against the light, which helps to dramatise the contrast between the earth and the translucent texture of grass.

113/114. Sheep leave their mark on the rural scene. Their many tracks radiate out from the watering hole on 114, while in the other picture a circular pattern is created by their movement around a small hill.

115/116. Dams leave their own peculiar imprints on farming land. To me these two examples take on a human character.

117/118. Two circular irrigation systems. 117 shows only a segment of the total circle that it covers. Water is pumped from the centre through a large pipe in a radial spraying system that is used for the growing of vegetables in the south-west. The other picture shows irrigation of red soil in the Kimberley.

119/120. The Ord River irrigation scheme utilises the abundance of water from Lake Kununurra and Lake Argyle. This, and the fertility of the fine black soil, enables the growing of a wide variety of crops, as seen from the air in these two photographs.

121/122. These patterns are from market gardens near Perth, growing vegetables on a smaller scale. The diversity of their crops can be seen in photograph 121. In 122, the preparation of the ground includes the laying of plastic sheeting over the soil, to contain weeds and to maximise moisture.

123. Paddocks are separated by a line of trees in what is otherwise a very denuded and barren landscape. These inland areas depend very much on the annual rainfall for their survival.

124. Although it gives the appearance of a similar situation as photograph 123, this is actually the base of an oil tank. The rivets that join the metal sheets and the residue of oil give the appearance of an aerial landscape.

125. Ballooning is a gentler way of obtaining aerial photographs. An unobstructed view gives more scope for the selection of a subject than from an aircraft. The disadvantage is that you have minimal control of the direction to be taken. This unpredictability makes every balloon journey truly a "flight of discovery."

126/127. There are a number of saltworks in Western Australia. 126 shows a truck crossing one of the dams at Dampier. The patterning on the water has been caused by wind. 127. Lake McLeod, north of Carnarvon, lies tranquil in early morning light. Its still waters show perfect cloud reflections.

128. More traces of man the measurer. Farm fence on a salt lake recoiling under the impact of time.

129. Polythene piping is very much a part of the modern Australian garden reticulation system. Here it measures its dose of water on young saplings along the Freeway.

130. Man's markings on the land. Doing "wheelies" on a salt lake leaves these circular patterns.

131. Chalk-like diagram left by geologists to site the limits of a gold deposit at Coolgardie.

132. In the iron ore industry huge amounts of waste have to be removed to get down to the ore deposit. This aerial shows one of those waste dumps situated in the Pilbara.

133. Like a giant Meccano set, equipment waiting to be assembled at the Burrup Peninsula LNG Plant.

134. Alumina processing plant waste is pumped into residue ponds, which from the air, provide a very colourful and abstract image.

135. Bench marks of an iron ore quarry, coast of Cockatoo Island.

136. Yachts waiting to be launched for an afternoon's sailing at one of Perth's Swan River yacht clubs.

137. Sunset over yachts at Success Harbour in Fremantle.

138. The markings of man's playgrounds – tennis versus basketball courts.

139. Suburban housing. Precise and repetitive, like a series of clones from a production line.

140/141. Two resting places – for man and his machines. The symmetry of the cemetery contrasts with the jumbled colours in a wrecker's car yard.

142. This large gathering of people on a festive occasion seems to have lost the identity of its individuals in a sea of colour.

I wish to thank the following people for their
assistance in the production of the book:

Janet Holmes à Court

Ray Van Kempen

Anne Ameling

Bill Warnock

also:

Jerome Lawler

George Seddon

John Douglas

Ray Coffey of Fremantle Centre Press

and the many pilots I have flown with
over the years, including:
Geoff Johnson, Scott Jorgensen, Ian Reid,
Susan Ward, Dennis Sarson, Don Phillips, Kerry Slingsby.

The images in this book
are as I've found them in the natural
landscape. There has been no
technical enhancement.
I use a variety of films and
cameras to suit the situation
and keep it as simple as
possible so I can concentrate
on the 'seeing.'

Sandpiper Press • Perth • Western Australia